Never Doubt Your Value
You Are More Than Enough!

DAWN J EPTING

Unmarked Scripture references or Scriptures marked "KJV" are taken from the King James Version of the Bible.
Scripture references from the Bible marked "NIV" (New International Version), "NKJV" (New King James Version), and "NLT" (New Living Translation) are taken from www.blueletterbible.org online.

Used by permission.

Never Doubt Your Value: You Are More Than Enough!

ISBN 978-0578981826

Copyright © 2021 Dawn J Epting Inc.

Website: www.dawnepting.com

All rights reserved. No part of this publication may be reproduced, stored in a retrieval system, or transmitted in any form or by any means, electronic, mechanical, photocopying, recording, or otherwise, without the prior written permission of the publisher.

Printed in the United States of America

This book is dedicated to anyone with a good heart who has ever questioned their value or self-worth due to being rejected, criticized, or ostracized. May you always remember that your value has never been in question and will forever be immeasurable!

TABLE OF CONTENTS

Introduction		vii
1	You Are Complete!	1
2	You Are Not Your Past!	17
3	You Are Creative!	31
4	You Are Not Rejected!	46
5	You Are Righteous!	66
6	You Are A Visionary!	77
7	You Are A Co-Creator!	89
8	You Already Are . . .	100
Notes		103
About The Author		109
Book Summary		111

INTRODUCTION

Life by its very nature has a way of causing us to question our inherent worth and value. This often begins in childhood, as was my experience. Often, our awareness of our value is obscured by years of enduring criticism, rejection, self-doubt, past regret, shame, and even self-condemnation. Your high value has always existed and has never fluctuated, but it is your awareness of that value that you may slowly be discovering. All of the diamonds, precious metals, and gems of the earth do not even begin to come close to your value that can be encapsulated in one statement, "You are more than enough!" Honestly, the full magnitude of your brilliance and splendor have yet to be unveiled. They have yet to be unveiled, not only to the world but to you as well. If we ever begin to grasp the full magnitude of what has been deposited on the inside of us, there will be no limits to what we can receive in terms of financial abundance, career success, thriving relationships, and physical well-being. In fact, those things will manifest effortlessly!

Often, we assess our value based on the circumstances in which we find ourselves or our stature in life. We often internalize the opinions of family members, authority figures, and peers concerning our value based on their distorted perceptions. These opinions cause us to question our value and our worthiness to pursue our dreams and receive life's best. Images abound in print media, on television, and on social media of what success embodies and what constitutes beauty. When we fail to measure up to the social images that have been presented, we further question our value and our worthiness, which further hinders our ability to receive our heart's desires. We fail to grasp that by virtue of our very existence and birth, we are more than enough.

If at some point we have been aware of our value, we may question if it remains intact when we make poor decisions, make mistakes, and fail to live up to our own expectations or the expectations of others. Decisions we have made in the past replay repeatedly on the film of our mind, filling us with guilt or shame and causing us to believe that the essence of who we are has somehow been diminished. We fail to comprehend that at the lowest points of our life and even when we have made the most questionable choices, our worth remains high, our value remains unscathed, and we are still worthy to experience the best that life has to offer.

A reprogramming must occur to remind us of who we are and have always been at our very core and essence, a reconditioning that unearths the inner brilliance that has been buried beneath the rigors and vicissitudes of life. You have the creative power to unleash your potential and experience the life of your dreams. May the words that follow be like a fresh wind that revives your entire being, allowing you to give yourself permission to value your existence, envision your dreams, and tackle your goals where you once may have felt underserving.

You have gifts and talents that the world stands in need of as you come into a greater and greater realization of who you have always been. You can envision your heart's desires and feel them as an accomplished fact, because they are indeed a done deal now. As you become more and more aware of who you have always been, you will experience your heart's desires. All things are literally possible for you. The question is not if you are valuable; the real question is, will you choose to see that value and walk in the reality of unlimited possibilities that have been made available to you?

1

YOU ARE COMPLETE!

You're worthy of greatness, even if you don't see it yet.

—Lauren Jarvis-Gibson

Life is not so much about obtaining as it is about discovering. Discovering that which you have been looking for externally but have always possessed internally! Once you discover what you possess inside, you will effortlessly receive all of life's abundance instead of striving hard to obtain it. When you truly awaken to who you are and have always been, there will be no limits to what you can receive in terms of abundance in relationships, finances, health, business endeavors, or dreams.

Success is indeed your birthright. You have a right to success, love, prosperity, health, and wholeness by virtue of birth alone and not based on anything you do, right or wrong. In fact, all things related to success, love, prosperity, and wholeness are already deposited on the inside of you. All of the gems and precious stones that the earth possesses cannot compare to your immeasurable value, for you were individually crafted and fashioned before the foundation of the world to be a unique masterpiece that embodies the image and likeness of the Divine One Himself. Your value is encapsulated in the fact that you are Divine. The same power that created worlds resides on the inside of you. Divinity is your true identity! In fact, royalty is also your identity. Measuring yourself as anything less than divine is sinful. Sin is not about the "wrong" outward actions you commit but entails not understanding who you truly are at the core of your being and mistakenly believing that there is something defective about you.

According to the Hebrew Lexicon, to sin is to miss the mark.[1] Failing to see your identity as divine is missing the mark, because the measurement of who you are is the Anointed One Himself. Not valuing ourselves as perpetually complete and enough solely by virtue of being divine or created in the image and likeness of God is sin. Outward "sinful" or fear-based behaviors occur when we fail to realize who we are and try to obtain by effort what is already ours by birth and inheritance. We have immense value simply by virtue of birth. The more we discover that we are and have always been more than enough, the more wealth, sound relationships, success, and physical well-being will flow to us effortlessly in life. Knowing the truth will set you free!

Truth that is truth has always been eternal truth and simply resonates on the inside of you. You were deeply loved and in the heart and mind of God before you physically came forth. Your origins go much further back than your physical birth on this earth. While we are often taught that our origins began with the Biblical Account of the creation of man in the Garden of Eden, our origins began before the foundation of the world. Ephesians 1:4 explains that "He chose us in Him before the foundation of the world" (NKJV). In fact, some theologians have espoused that from eternities past, we were with the Creator in pure spirit form. Since we came out of the Eternal One, having been in Him in pure spirit form from eternities past makes sense. Spirit is infinite, limitless, and of course eternal. Spirit transcends the constraints of time and space. As an infinite spiritual being, you were therefore complete before birth, are complete now, and will always be complete, despite what circumstances may try to suggest to you. There is no past and no future with Spirit, because all exists now. Every solution and resource has been deposited on the inside of you and is available to you right this instant.

Since you were in God before the foundation of the world and are perpetually in the eternal now, the solution to every challenge you may be facing and every resource you are in need of have already been provided and are available for you to tap into right now. You have access to every resource right now solely on the basis of your identity. You have always been and will always be unconditional love, joy, peace, wholeness, and prosperity. You need not ever search outside of yourself to find these things in other people or circumstances, because those things have always and will always reside on the inside of you. In fact, the more that you search for these things in outward people or circumstances, the more these things may seem to elude you, and the more those people and the circumstances you desire may be pushed away from you.

Your immeasurable value has always existed from eternities past and will exist throughout all eternity. The true essence of who you will always be is an eternal spirit, complete before birth with infinite worth and value, regardless of circumstances or your behavior. In recent years, much has been made about manifesting your desires, but if you are trying to manifest out of a heart without the knowledge of your inherent worth and value, you may never walk in the experience of the abundant life you were created to enjoy. Additionally, many self-help books written today beseech you to obtain by performance or effort that which is already yours by virtue of creation and design. While it is great to flow in your gifts and talents and consequently make a living, you were never designed to toil. By virtue of being a son (or daughter), you have an inheritance not based on performance. The key to effortlessly receiving your inheritance lies in delving deep into an understanding of your true identity!

The Origins of Sin (Mistaken Identity)

Throughout time, those who understood who they were went on to do great things in life. Conversely, those who did not understand their identity often fell short of their dreams and goals. In the account of Adam and Eve, for example, the couple partook of the tree of the knowledge of good and evil because they were told by the serpent, "When you eat from it your eyes will be opened, and you will be like God, knowing good and evil" (Genesis 3:5 NIV). The implication to the man and woman by the serpent was that they were not enough or not complete as they had already been created and that they had to do something by effort to obtain completion. The implication was also that they had to have their "eyes opened" or judge by external appearance what is "good" and what is "bad," instead of being led to their highest good from within.

Partaking of the tree of the knowledge of good and evil consists of trying to obtain by effort that which externally appears to be good and shunning what we perceive as evil. The man and the woman tried to obtain the "good" of being like God or being worthy and in the process were shunning the "evil" of not being like God or being incomplete based on what they perceived with their five physical senses. The truth was that they were already like God, created in His image, complete, loved, and already enough, but they were unaware of their true identity!

Partaking of the wrong tree, namely the tree of the knowledge of good and evil, always results in death, even today. This is not necessarily a physical death but loss in whatever area of our lives we employ it.

Anytime we attempt to do something in our own strength to obtain a "favorable" result or judge a situation as evil by surface appearances such as Adam and Eve did, we are in mistaken identity (sin) and producing death.

Often, we believe that not possessing certain things says something about our worth and value. We can even be in mistaken identity or sin when we try to manifest as many people are doing because they believe the manifestation will make them feel more whole and complete. We are already complete and need nothing outside of ourselves to make us more complete. While we can enjoy external things, we do not need them to be complete. Allowing the senses to dictate that we must obtain by effort that which is already ours by birthright (wholeness) never lasts, even if we are pursuing something that is "good."

The tree of the knowledge of good and evil is a simultaneous performing in our own strength to get the good and judging and resisting the evil based on sensory perception or external circumstances.

Trying to perform to get the good never lasts but brings death, and opposing the evil only causes it to persist because we are focusing on the evil and bringing more of it into our awareness and ultimately experience.

Partaking of this tree occurs when we allow external stimuli to determine our internal inherent worth and value! The knowledge of good and evil always brings death (or loss) in whatever area of our life we employ it. We are to see life in all situations and circumstances we find ourselves in and simply rest in knowing that we are whole and complete within!

For example, a person who believes they will obtain value or have significance by working hard to get a promotion at work may be eating from the tree of the knowledge of good and evil—the wrong tree. While there is nothing wrong with desiring a promotion, we should not seek it to feel whole or complete. Although getting the promotion may look good, that person is trying to obtain something outside of themselves by effort that they already intrinsically are—someone of value. They are also simultaneously judging themself as invaluable and producing more of the feeling of worthlessness in the process.

Eating of the wrong tree can also entail not believing we are whole because we lack money, are not in a relationship, or have been diagnosed with some illness. All of these sensory-based perceived limitations may cause us to obtain by effort the finances, relationship, or health that we feel we lack in order to make us feel whole while simultaneously shunning the lack of money, solitude, or ill health that we allow to make us feel inadequate. We are always whole, despite conditions or circumstances. In some form or another, we probably all eat or have eaten of the tree of the knowledge of good and evil's corruptible, perishable fruit. While we may obtain the sensory-based thing(s) that we feel we lack or desire temporarily, these temporary conditions usually do not last. In fact, even if we do obtain the money, relationship, or healing we desire in the sensory realm, we still may not feel complete and may ultimately lose those things, because true wholeness comes only from within. We must not seek fleeting temporary changes to make us feel valuable, but we must realize our eternal value. Whether it is lack in our finances, sickness in our physical body, or the failure of relationships, eating of the tree of the knowledge of good and evil brings death. The tree of the knowledge of good and evil screams for us to take action based on the sensory realm, whereas the Tree of Life constantly whispers, "You Already Are."

The Tree of Life
The Tree of Life is the understanding that "I Already Am," despite outward appearances or regardless of what it looks like in the sensory realm. It is also understanding our union with God. It is the understanding that we do

not have to judge outward situations and circumstances but that we remain perpetually righteous. Many religions have been guilty of eating from the tree of the knowledge of good and evil. In essence, their followers have been taught to strive by performance to obtain good standing with God while simultaneously shunning outward "sinful" behavior.

Trying to perform is often temporary because they continue to fall short of human-derived standards of perfection, never feel complete enough, and judging and shunning "sinful" behavior actually often produces more of the behavior they don't want, which brings self-condemnation and ultimately death.

Contrary to popular belief, man was created and has always been complete and whole. There is nothing to obtain by effort and nothing to judge or shun. The only thing that limits us from walking in the experience of our completeness in our sensory external experience is our lack of understanding that "I Already Am" and simply resting in that awareness in all circumstances. Once we understand internally who we already are, external things will begin to be unveiled or manifest effortlessly in terms of the finances, relationships, wholeness in health, and the other prosperity we seek.

You Already are!

We are created in the image and likeness of Almighty God. When Moses asked God in Exodus 3:13 who he should tell the people of Israel sent him to deliver them, God replied, "I AM THAT I AM." Similarly, concerning yourself, you must meditate on the realization that "I Already Am." Regardless of what it looks like you may lack, "You Already Are."

In fact, the Scriptures record that "the kingdom of God is within you" (Luke 17:21). Jesus made the preceding statement and walked in the "I Already Am" principle and righteousness and was able to receive limitlessly from God. Jesus understood that He was complete on the inside with no need of anything from the outside. He understood His oneness with the Father. Jesus did not only come FOR us but AS us. Consequently, we too can receive limitlessly from God.

Tree of Life living entails walking in your "I AM-ness" or union with the Father. Jesus walked in a strong conviction of who He was without doubt, guilt, fear, shame, self-condemnation, or any other limitation. Whenever there was a perceived financial or physical need in someone's life, it was met effortlessly for Jesus. Similarly, everything you will ever need has already been deposited on the inside of you, like it was for Jesus. You are not in need of finances; you already are abundance. You are not waiting for physical healing; you already are wholeness. You are not seeking love; you already are love personified. You already are! You must learn to simply be! The more you meditate and feel the fact that you already are in every area of life, the more your desires will manifest on the outside. Your desires may be for things in your own life or desires for healing, wholeness, and increase in the lives of those around you.

It has been written that "hope deferred makes the heart sick, but when the desire comes, it is a Tree of Life" (Proverbs 13:12 NKJV). Hoping, waiting, and wondering when and if a desire will be fulfilled leads to discouragement and sometimes even depression. Meditating on the fact that "You Already Are" whatever you desire and allowing yourself to feel the reality of the desire now, despite appearances, is what Tree of Life living is all about. In fact, the Scriptures encourage us to believe that we have already received our desires when we pray or meditate and they will be ours (Mark 11:24).

The Quadriplegic Gymnast's Miracle

Miracles occur when we meditate and feel the truth of who we already are. The word miracle can be defined as "an effect or extraordinary event in the physical world that surpasses all known human or natural powers and is ascribed to a supernatural cause."[2]

Take Lindsey Schuler for example. According to an article in *USA Today*, Lindsey was an Indiana high school cheerleader who sustained a spinal cord injury during a practice in 2016.[3] Lindsey was lying on the gym floor immediately after the accident but was unable to move anything from the neck down, according to the article. Something interesting happened, though.

"At that moment, lying on a gym floor . . . Schuler did something remarkable. She became thankful for what she had, and she started visualizing what it FELT like to walk and flip and twist. 'In my mind,' said Schuler, 'I could always still feel'"[4]. Needless to say, Lindsey Schuler was able to walk not long after her accident and in fact took steps at her prom a few weeks later. Lindsey did not judge her accident as evil or try to obtain healing by force. Lindsey also did not meditate on self-condemning thoughts such as, "I should not have attempted that back handspring move that resulted in my current paralysis," or "my gymnastics mistake is the reason I'm in this situation and paralyzed." She simply gave thanks for what she could still feel, stood in the realization of who she was on the inside, and healing and wholeness had to manifest on the outside. When we meditate on our wholeness, we do not have to attempt to get healed; it simply manifests as a byproduct of who we already are!

Dr. Joe Dispenza's Healing

World-renowned speaker and *New York Times* bestselling author, Dr. Joe Dispenza, had a similar experience to Lindsey Schuler's. Dr. Dispenza "started out as a chiropractor, earning his doctor of chiropractic degree from Life University in Atlanta, GA. He had a successful chiropractic practice, but one day, he had a dangerous accident. In 1986, while cycling in a triathlon, Dr. Joe was hit by a truck. He broke six vertebrae in his spine, and his doctors told him he would never walk again."[5]

In many of his teachings, Dr. Dispenza explains how the doctors encouraged him to have a surgery that would relieve some of his pain, though they believed he would still never walk again. Dr. Dispenza decided to take a different route. Instead, "Dr. Joe refused to have the surgery and began to imagine himself totally healed. He visualized each vertebrae healing and reconstructed his spine in his mind. In just ten and a half weeks, Dr. Joe was back on his feet, and in twelve weeks, he was training again and back at work at his chiropractic clinic."[6] Dr. Dispenza visualized the end he desired without trying to perform to obtain it!

It is also important for us to focus on what we want as opposed to what we don't want in our lives as Dr. Dispenza did. When we judge something as bad and focus on it, it have a tendency to produce more of what we don't want in our lives. Whatever we focus on has a way of materializing in our life. Essentially, whatever we focus on grows. Like Dr. Joe, we are to focus on our desired goal knowing that we "already are" and not focus on the perceived sickness, lack, or thing we do not desire.

A person who is experiencing symptoms of an illness, for example, may be praying words of healing, while still being fearful, seeing themselves as sick, and believing they are unworthy to experience healing and wholeness. Like Lindsey and Dr. Dispenza, we should not condemn ourselves for being in the situations we find unwanted or obtain healing by effort but should simply visualize the outcome we desire knowing that we are already complete.

As a Man Thinks, so is He

We are to visualize the end we desire and feel its reality, because it is indeed already an accomplished fact! Whatever you focus on will inevitably show up in your reality. There are literally infinite possibilities in terms of the life you can experience. The Scriptures state that as a man thinketh in his heart, so is he (Proverbs 23:7) or so will his experience be. Your life will go in the direction of your most dominant thought, because where attention goes, energy flows. You will experience your dominant thoughts and feelings.

We meditate on or visualize the life we desire not to make it so but because it already is so. All things have been given to us (2 Peter 1:3), and all possibilities exists now, because all things are possible. Meditation should not involve toil but should be fun. The moment we feel like we are toiling to make our desire come to pass, we have gotten into self-effort. Meditation involves seeing, feeling, hearing, smelling, and tasting the thrill of the desire that has been placed in our heart as a reality. It is resting in the peace and satisfaction of knowing that our desire is an accomplished fact because we "already are!"

2

YOU ARE NOT YOUR PAST!

*It is time to stop punishing yourself for past failures,
and to stop beating yourself in the present.*

—Carlton Rivers

Past programming and experiences often cause us to doubt our inherent worth and value. Too often, this doubt about our value stems from past events and statements from others. Our past may cause us to question if we currently are more than enough. It can also cause us to doubt if we are worthy to experience the desires of our heart. Experts generally agree that most of our early programming occurs from birth up until the age of seven. Noted biologist and epigeneticist Bruce Lipton teaches extensively about the importance of reprogramming our subconscious mind as adults due to potential negative early life programming in his various online video teachings and lectures.

Lipton states, "We learned our programs in the first seven years of life. During this time, the mind is operating in a low vibrational frequency like hypnosis. The theta state is very receptive."[7] As adults, our subconscious minds are in the theta frequency immediately before drifting off to sleep and immediately upon waking up. This is why the best times to visualize and feel the reality of experiencing your desires are right before bed and immediately upon waking up, according to experts, because these are the times the subconscious can be more easily programmed. Children, however, are in a constant state of theta for the first seven years of their lives according to Lipton, which is the reason children are impressionable and easily programmed all the time. They are receptive to the positive or negative suggestions by those around them and tend to easily internalize the suggestions of others.

As children, we willingly and without resistance accept the thoughts, ideas, and suggestions that are given to us by our parents, teachers, authority figures, peers, and other influencers. The ideas that are conveyed to us by authority figures during our early years are known as heterosuggestion, or suggestions from outside of ourselves. Heterosuggestion can be defined as "suggestions from another person," according to Joseph Murphy in his book, *The Power of Your Subconscious Mind*.[8]

As we become aware of outside suggestions, we must learn to guard our hearts and minds from outside suggestions and influences that are contrary to our eternal divine and spiritual identity. Any suggestion from outside of you that implicitly or explicitly states that you are incomplete does not need to be entertained or dwelled upon. You do not have to accept the thoughts and opinions of others as your own and can immediately reject them. If we are not careful, external suggestions of incompleteness can be internalized and take up residence in our hearts. Repeated negative suggestions from our past can create subconscious patterns and unhealthy suggestions on the inside of us well into our adult life that run on autopilot known as autosuggestion. Autosuggestion can take the form of "silent fear thoughts emotionalized and subjectified," according to Joseph Murphy.[9]

Deeply entrenched fear-based programming that we are deficient in some way can run on autopilot, create repeated fear patterns, and become the basis from which we navigate life. Left unchecked and unquestioned, incorrect programming from our past may later result in a host of problems, maladies, and insecurities in various areas of life.

Getting to The Root

It is well known that a tree's fruit or leaves are only as good as its root system. A tree with good roots will produce good fruit, and conversely, a tree with bad or corrupt roots will produce bad fruit or results. The fruit we produce in terms of understanding our identity will only be as good as the seeds that have been planted to affirm who we are.

As previously noted in terms of subconscious conditioning, our roots—so to speak—are formed during early childhood from birth to approximately seven years of age, based on the seeds that are planted during that time. The roots are analogous with our perception of our identity. Condemnation from critical statements, emotional abuse, or rejection in our childhood can result in negative subconscious programming, self-hatred, perpetual cycles of rejection, and subpar results (fruit) in our lives. Condemning statements and behavior from authority figures early in life may take root and cause us to question our adequacy and value. Young children who are excessively criticized or punished often develop roots of shame and self-condemnation, which is not who they are!

In his book *Destined to Reign*, Pastor Joseph Prince discusses the deepest impediment to receiving God's grace and abundance in life. Prince notes, "If you were growing a plant, and the plant was getting weak and sickly, it would be foolish to attempt to nourish and restore the plant by dealing with superficial elements such as its leaves. To resolve the problem, you would have to go after its roots."[10] The root of negative behavior patterns, continued cycles of defeat, or impediments to receiving God's best in life always need to be addressed.

Prince goes on to state, "When you are able to identify and deal with the root, the fruit and the leaves—or the outward manifestations—will take care of themselves," and that the deepest root or hindrance to manifesting the abundant life that God intended for us to experience is "condemnation."[11] Critical statements made by others that often start in childhood as well as abuse we have endured plant self-condemning seeds in our hearts, and those seeds take root if we allow them to. We mistakenly grow up believing that we are unworthy of nurturing relationships, abundant finances, or wholeness in our health, not realizing that all those things have already been provided for us and are available to us by virtue of our birth.

In childhood, we are also mistakenly taught that "good" performance results in rewards or being blessed and "bad" performance results in punishment or loss. This negative programming causes us later in life to strive to obtain by effort what has already been made available by grace. We try to perform to obtain the good things in life, because we have deep-rooted self-condemnation and fear that we are not deserving or good enough. Essentially, we run our lives on faulty programming. In many instances, this fear-based programming took root at some point during our youth and is reinforced by social norms and those closest to us as we navigate through life.

If you take a moment to think back long and hard enough, chances are that you will remember specific instances that caused you to develop a belief that you currently hold, good or bad. If you currently struggle in a particular area of your life—whether it is relationally, physically, or financially—there was probably a negative seed that was planted somewhere in your past. These seeds take root and are constantly growing, producing fruit in our lives.

The seeds planted early in life become our practiced vibration or our persistent mode of thinking and feeling and consequently dominant frequency or point of attraction.

Practicing the vibration you have practiced for years is what is producing the current results in your life experience. We are to practice and resonate a guilt-free vibration. I can remember being teased by an aunt and my peers about certain aspects of my physical appearance as a child. Unknowingly, I allowed those damaging statements (seeds) to take root in my heart and mind to the extent that I believed my appearance had to be "perfect" in order to "qualify" to have friends and good relationships later in life. Essentially, I did not believe I was enough and often fell short of attaining the friendships and relationships I desired.

I can also remember being told that I did certain things "wrong" by a particular family member early in life, even though I did not. Those early false accusations caused me to shoulder blame for things in relationships later in life that I had not done and practice thoughts and feelings of guilt, shame, and unworthiness. Anytime something went wrong in a relationship, I believed that I was the sole cause of its failure, somehow. I falsely believed that my behavior was wrong in some way and that I was not enough, which led to striving to perform better, people pleasing, and ultimately death (the relationships failing, anyway).

Walk Free From Condemnation

If we are not careful, harboring self-condemnation from the past can lead to unhealthy attachments to people, the need for their affirmation, and loss of true identity. As the founder of a crisis hotline that received hundreds of calls after its implementation, I have seen the detrimental effects of people harboring self-condemnation from their past into their present. Self-condemnation often leads to feelings of depression, anxiety, or even suicide. Condemnation will zap your physical energy, produce emotional turmoil, and deplete your zeal for life.

Whenever we try to manifest relationships or anything else we desire out of fear or condemnation, they will ultimately fail.

At times, we may even sabotage the things we presently desire by practicing the fear-based vibration of our past. We may enter a good relationship but believe it is too good to be true, that we don't deserve it, and sabotage it, causing it to fail. We must realize that we are worthy of receiving great relationships, good friendships, financial abundance, and wholeness in our physical bodies simply by virtue of our existence. The right seeds must begin to be planted and must take root in our heart. We don't need to uproot incorrect past belief systems per se, but we must begin to plant the correct beliefs about who we truly are into our heart. Light is what dispels darkness, not trying to uproot it. Knowing the truth is what sets us free (John 8:32)! As the correct seeds are planted, incorrect ones will naturally be uprooted, and we will walk in the experience of God's abundance in life. The Kingdom of God is often compared to a tiny seed in the Scriptures (Mark 4:26 & Matthew 13:31) that produces a great harvest. We can experience the full manifestation of the goodness of God by simply planting small seeds of His love, His goodness, and our righteous standing in Him in our heart and not dwelling on the negative events of our past. If we do not start planting the right seeds and beliefs, our past can potentially sabotage the things we desire to experience in our lives. Feel free to speak the following exercise aloud concerning your righteousness, despite past situations and circumstances.

- My parent passed away = I am righteous
- I have a sexually transmitted disease (STD) from the past = I am righteous

- I have been divorced = I am righteous
- I had an abortion = I am righteous
- I had a child as a teenager = I am righteous
- I have been rejected by someone = I am righteous
- I was bullied as a child = I am righteous
- I have no money due to past decisions = I am righteous

Concerning your present circumstance, you might make the following statements that express your right standing, despite circumstances.

- I am unemployed = I am righteous
- I have breast cancer = I am righteous
- My spouse or significant other left me = I am righteous
- I have never been married like I wanted = I am righteous
- I have never had children like I wanted = I am righteous
- My boss is treating me unkindly = I am righteous
- The people on my job don't like me = I am righteous
- My family excludes me = I am righteous

- My mom or dad has always been mean to me = I am righteous

I know the preceding exercise might seem counterintuitive, but it is the truth of who you are. You are not your past! In fact, you are not even the current negative or fear-based behavior you may be exhibiting. Essentially, it does not matter what state you may be or have been in, your perpetual eternal identity is righteous. It is important to internalize this truth of righteousness, because God makes it clear that we reign in life through receiving an abundance of grace and the gift of righteousness (Romans 5:17).

Jesus walked in righteousness and was able to receive limitlessly from God. He was able to multiply bread and loaves from heaven, heal the sick, and even calm the sea. Jesus knew He was righteous and had no guilt of any kind. He was not fazed by the many condemning statements that the Pharisees and teachers of religious law hurled at Him. He understood His true identity and righteousness. As He is so are we. We too are to understand our true identity in order to receive all the best of God.

It does not matter how much we are told or feel that we have fallen short in the past, we remain perpetually righteous and can experience new life. So-called "wrong" behavior does not determine our identity or destiny. In fact, our "wrong" past behavior does not even exist in God's sight. The Bible states that "I will never again remember their sins" (Hebrews 8:12 NLT). That means God is not remembering your past, so you should not remember your past either! Everything is now (in the present moment) with God. There is no past or future with God, since He resides outside of time in eternity.

Your Recreated Past!

Your "past" can also literally be rewritten or recreated! Michael (Mike) Popovich, Pastor at Freedom Ministries in Colorado Springs, Colorado, has shared a story multiple times during his online services about him and his wife Barb. He talks about the fact that they had marital difficulties early in their marriage and about how they decided to rewrite their past, so to speak, to improve their marital challenges. They met as adults but started saying that they were high school sweethearts. That story undoubtedly started embedding the belief in Pastor Mike's and his wife's heart that they had been the love of each other's lives for many years. As a result, their marriage began to improve and is strong to this day. They literally rewrote the story of their past, felt the feeling of being in love for years, and it affected their present-day reality in a positive manner.

The parable of the unrighteous servant in Luke 16 of the Bible is also the story of rewriting pasts, according to Pastor Mike in a couple of his sermons.[12] The unrighteous servant reduced the debts of some of his master's debtors. The debtors were no longer required to pay what they owed the master, and their bills were rewritten so they could pay much less. Essentially, the servant rewrote the debt of their past. You do not have to dwell on every thought that comes to your mind, including thoughts about your past. Our present reality is being formed every instant based on the thoughts we think NOW.

Our past has no bearing on our present or even future. Refrain from judging your past. All of it was good and brought you to where you are today. There are no mistakes in life per se, since everything is good and working out for our ultimate good. All things are just growth opportunities—opportunities to calibrate to who we really are.

Reality is pliable and bendable, so any situation can be changed at any time. We can either choose to rewrite what we define as negative past experiences or reframe them. With cognitive reframing, we can choose to assign positive meaning to past experiences, since situations inherently have no meaning anyway except for the meaning we assign them. If we perpetually think on past experiences from a negative perspective, we will recreate the same experience we do not desire in our present-day reality. We do not have to live bound to our past. We can create the abundant life we presently desire by seeing ourselves as righteous with a bright future. Remember that you can see your past in a positive light in order to affect change in your present.

We have the ability to change our present reality at any time by not judging our past. Our past is irrelevant. All that exists is NOW! Christ stands outside of time, and all we desire is available to us NOW! If we think new, uplifting thoughts of life and allow ourselves to experience good emotions daily, we will create different positive experiences instead of the negative experiences we don't want. You are the only thinker in your universe and can choose to think thoughts that mold and shape your present reality for the better.

3

YOU ARE CREATIVE!

Everything you can imagine is real.

—Pablo Picasso

Our thoughts are creative! This is a simple statement but a profound one. An inspired thought has a way of flooding our entire being with peace, and that thought has the power to produce change in our life as we meditate on it. We are to be led by the still small voice inside of us as we are led to transform our lives into an abundant one. You have the power in this instant to shape your reality based on your thoughts. Like Dorothy in *The Wizard of Oz,* who finally realized that the power always was within her to get back home to Kansas, the power has always resided in you to create the life you desire because you have been gifted with that ability.

It has often been said that thoughts become things. Again, Scripture is clear that "as a man thinketh in his heart, so is he" (Proverbs 23:7). You are what you think! Your reality today is a direct result of the thoughts you thought yesterday. Reality is shaped by our thoughts. The outer reality is always a byproduct of our inner thoughts and feelings. More specifically, the way we inwardly feel about ourselves affects how we experience outer reality. If the thoughts we have about ourselves and others are positive and uplifting, we will tend to experience an abundant and prosperous reality filled with love and gratitude. Conversely, if the thoughts we have are negative and self-degrading, the reality we experience may be less than ideal.

The only reason you ever have negative thoughts and emotions and consequently have what you interpret as "negative" life experiences is because your thoughts and heart are not aligned with who you really are, which is worthy and more than enough. In fact, as far as our health is concerned, negative and self-degrading thoughts about who we are may contribute to poor health and sickness in our bodies. Jesus made it a point in the ninth chapter of Matthew to forgive a paralyzed man's sins before healing him. In essence, healing is often linked to having a righteousness consciousness about ourselves and understanding our inherent worthiness. Fear, guilt, anger, shame, and self-condemnation keeps emotions trapped in our bodies and have a tendency to creep into our reality, often as the manifestation of physical ailments, disease, and other limitations. Our thoughts are powerful, and our lives tend to go in the direction of our most dominant thought, relationally, financially, and even physically.

Life is about the stories we constantly tell ourselves. If we constantly tell ourselves stories such as "I could never finish college," or "I could never start a business," or "I am too old to try something new," or "People will not want to do business with me," for example, those stories will become a reality in our lives.

It has been estimated by some experts that the average person has approximately 50,000 thoughts per day. Most of these thoughts occur very rapidly due to entrenched programming and run almost on autopilot. In essence, often, we have the same repeated thought patterns before we are even aware of them. These repeated thought patterns (autosuggestion) produce the same experiences in our lives over and over. It has also been stated that our emotions are often an indication of the thoughts we are thinking. If we are feeling depleted or depressed, for example, it would be wise for us to ask ourselves, "What am I thinking?"

We should not dwell on thoughts about what is wrong or impossible in our lives. We should not even dwell on thoughts about what is possible for us based on another person's similar experience. In essence, we should not limit what is possible in our lives based on the outcome of someone else's experience in a similar situation. Two different people can be given the same medical diagnosis, for example, but experience very different outcomes in their physical health based on their individual thoughts and emotions. One person might have an outcome they don't desire, while the other person experiences one that they do want.

The quickest and most efficient way to exact change in our external world is to change our inner reality. The outside is always simply a reflection of the inside. Teacher and author Kay Fairchild has often stated that when you're sitting in a movie theater, it appears that the movie is on the screen in front of you. She goes on to state that the movie is actually on film in the back room. What is inside of the back room simply projects onto the screen in front of the viewer. The same is true with our lives. What is on the film of our hearts and minds, so to speak, merely becomes a reality on the screen of space and time before us.

Another important truth to note is that nothing has any power in and of itself except for the power we assign to it or give it. We have usually empowered at some point everything that occurs in our lives. Our fear and attention to certain things are the precursors to what we interpret as "negative" events occurring in our life experience, and our love and appreciation of other things lead to what we define as "positive" events taking place in our life experience. Our thoughts, no one else's, is what produces results in our life! Whatever we focus on grows in our minds and consequently life.

It would behoove us to refrain from dwelling on the details of a problem we may be confronted with and only see our righteousness and life in every situation.

We are not to judge, shun, or fix by effort the things we do not want in our lives. We merely need to choose and focus on a different alternative (possibility) that we desire that fills us with peace and well-being. If we want to experience something new in our lives, we must change our thoughts and emotions.

Focus on Love and Life!
There is only one power in the entire universe. God is love (1 John 4:8) and our life (Colossians 3:4)! There is only

love and life. Whether we see it or not is our choice. There is no lesser or "evil" power that can unilaterally wreak havoc in your life, since it is already under your feet, anyway. What we judge, we empower. If we judge a situation—such as a health challenge or financial shortage, for example—as evil based on sensory perception and fear it, we empower it and often produce more of it in our lives. The only power is love and life. We are to focus on love and life. How we use the power we have been given determines the "good or bad" reality we experience. If we pinch off the love, life, and light that fills everything, we will experience darkness or the absence of light.

What we consider evil experiences are simply an absence of the awareness of the God life and power we have been given! In essence, darkness is the absence of light. Our experiences, whether "desirable" or "undesirable," are shaped by our thoughts and emotions. Thoughts and feelings that focus on that which is pure, lovely, and of good report lead to "good" experiences, while thoughts and feelings filled with fear, anger, self-condemnation, depression, worry, and stress often result in experiences that are not desirable.

In fact, fears harbored in the heart introduce unnecessary resistance to receiving the things we desire. Additionally, fear-based efforts to attain our desires introduce unnecessary resistance that limits the visible manifestation of what we desire in our lives. Thoughts and feelings of self-condemnation limit what we can possess and achieve in life, because we don't feel worthy to possess those things.

Whatever we give our attention to grows. Any "negative" situation is subject to change, anyway, as we align our thoughts and feelings to that which is lovely, pure, and of a good report (Philippians 4:8). We are to see life, the eternal, and what we desire in every situation in order to tap into the eternal flow of blessings we inherently possess.

Feel it Now

It has often been said that everything we desire in life is because we believe we will feel good as a result of possessing it. If we desire a financial fortune, companionship, or good health, for example, we believe that those things will result in good and uplifting feelings and emotions. If we desire healing and wholeness or financial freedom for someone else's life, we believe it will produce uplifting feelings and emotions in us as well. We can allow ourselves, however, to feel feelings of gratitude, love, and joy long before the physical manifestation of the things we desire. Allowing ourselves to have life-giving thoughts and feelings filled with love, gratitude, worthiness, and righteousness leads to the manifestation of abundance and prosperity in life. These uplifting thoughts and feelings are who we are and reflect our true nature and character.

We do not need conditions in our lives to change in order to practice these unconditional uplifting feelings!

If we can practice these unconditional feelings without the conditions changing, our circumstances are certain to change. If we choose to allow ourselves to dwell on self-condemning and fearful thoughts and feelings, however, we may continually experience things we don't desire in our lives. All things are literally possible (Mark 9:23). Every scenario that you can imagine and conceive of in your mind can become a reality in your life, ranging from abundance to lack. What you imagine or "image" in your mind, you produce in your life. We can change what is occurring in our life experience simply by changing our minds. Thoughts and emotions have a charge or vibration to them that attract things into our life experience. As stated earlier, our emotions are an indication of what we are thinking. Good emotions indicate good feeling thoughts of love, appreciation, or joy, for example, while bad emotions indicate inferior thoughts of hate, fear, or lack. We can feel the feelings of the outcome we desire now.

Pray Rain

In his book, *Secrets of The Lost Mode of Prayer*, Gregg Braden gives a powerful example of the importance of not judging a circumstance we do not desire as "evil" but simply aligning our thoughts and feelings with what we do desire in order to experience it. During a historic drought in New Mexico, Gregg and a Native American friend of his went out to the desert to "pray rain." His friend stepped into a circle, closed his eyes, and spent a few moments there but never "prayed." His friend simply "closed his eyes, his breathing became slow, and his body became motionless. After a few short moments, he took a deep breath and said, 'Let's go. Our work is finished here.' Gregg was shocked and asked are you going to pray for rain? His friend said 'No, I said that I would 'pray rain.' If I prayed for rain, it could never happen. Prayers for rain empower the drought. Continuing to ask for these things puts the feeling on the drought and not on the rain."[13]

Gregg asked him what he prayed, and he responded in the following way. He said, "I began to have the feeling of what rain feels like. I felt the feeling of rain on my body and what it feels like to stand with my naked feet in the mud of our village plaza, because there has been so much rain. I smelled the smells of rain on the earthen walls in our village and felt what it feels like to walk through fields of corn chest high because there has been so much rain. I then felt grateful for the opportunity to participate in creation. Through our thanks, we honor all possibilities, while bringing the ones we choose into the world."[14] Within a matter of hours after Gregg's friend prayed rain, it began to rain!

Essentially, praying from the stance of what we "don't have" (the drought in this case) only empowers more of what we don't have, while praying from the realization and feeling of the fact that we have already been given all things empowers more of what we desire in our lives and experience. Notice that Gregg's friend did not judge the drought as evil and try to obtain the good of rain by force. He simply prayed the feeling of what he desired, and that is what occurred. He prayed from the thoughts and feelings of what he desired and not from what he did not desire. What he saw on the inside was more real than what was on the outside to the point that he was no longer concerned about or focused on the external circumstance or drought at all. It was inconsequential. He already had the rain long before it manifested in the natural realm.

When we believe that we already have what we desire on the inside, we will no longer look for it on the outside, but it still has a way of effortlessly manifesting.

We have already been given all things and are worthy to receive them. We also already possess all things and are whole and complete. The power always resides within you to receive. Your power can be used for what you define as "good" or "evil." You can create the reality you desire with uplifting thoughts and feelings and the realization that you are worthy to receive it. It is your choice.

The Most Important Parable
We are implored in Mark 4:13 to understand a certain parable because then we will understand all of them. The parable is found below:

> Listen! A farmer went out to plant some seed. As he scattered it across his field, some of the seed fell on a footpath, and the birds came and ate it. Other seed fell on shallow soil with underlying rock. The seed sprouted quickly because the soil was shallow. But the plant soon wilted under hot sun, and since it didn't have deep roots, it died. Other seed fell among thorns that grew up and choked out the tender plants so they produced no grain. Still other seeds fell on fertile soil, and they sprouted, grew, and produced a crop that was

thirty, sixty, and even a hundred times as much as had been planted (Mark 4:3-8 NLT).

Below, Jesus explains the meaning of the parable to His disciples:

> You are permitted to understand **the secret** of the Kingdom of God. But I use parables for everything I say to outsiders, so that the Scriptures might be fulfilled: 'When they see what I do, they will learn nothing. When they hear what I say, they will not understand. Otherwise, they will turn to me and be forgiven.' Then Jesus said to them, if you can't understand the meaning of this parable, how will you understand all the other parables? The farmer plants seed by taking God's word to others. The seed that fell on the footpath represents those who hear the message, only to have Satan come at once and take it away. The seed on the rocky soil represents those who hear the message and immediately receive it with joy. But since they don't have deep roots, they don't last long. They fall away as soon as they have problems or are persecuted for believing God's word. The seed that fell among the thorns represents others who

hear God's word, but all too quickly the message is crowded out by the worries of this life, the lure of wealth, and the desire for other things, so no fruit is produced. And the seed that fell on good soil represents those who hear and accept God's word and produce a harvest of thirty, sixty, or even a hundred times as much as had been planted (Mark 4:11-20 NLT)!

There is a lot to unpack in this parable—the parable of the sower, as it is called. Verse eleven explains that there is a secret to tap into or experience the Kingdom of God. In the parable, the Kingdom is compared to planting seed in soil. There was seed that fell on a footpath, on rocky soil, among thorns, and on good soil. The soil is synonymous with the human heart. It only takes a small seed planted to produce a harvest. In human conception, for example, the invisible seed of a man is planted into the womb of a woman and ultimately produces a visible miraculous manifestation of human life or a birth.

Verse nine of the parable explains THE SECRET of the Kingdom. *The secret of the Kingdom is that whatever we plant in our heart grows up and produces fruit in our lives, no matter how small the seed.*

Rhonda Byrne's 2006 book, *The Secret*, was about this premise regarding how the seeds we plant produce a harvest in our lives. We can choose to plant good seeds that produce a fruitful life. The seed of God is incorruptible (1 Peter 1:23). It produces every time. The condition of the heart determines whether the seed will produce lasting fruit or the desires that have been placed in our heart in our life experience. A tiny seed itself produces without the need for human effort, as long as the heart is open, receptive, and rooted in its eternal value. We simply need to plant the seed and guard our heart. We don't have to make our dreams and desires come to pass; we only need to plant the seed in an open and receptive heart. While there are actions we may be led to take before our desire(s) appear, these actions will be done from a heart that is rested in its inherent righteousness and value apart from circumstances. We are also to rest in the fact that our desire is already an accomplished fact.

The deeper our hearts are rooted in our unchangeable eternal identity, the more permanent and perpetual the visible fruit we desire will be in our lives. Lack of being rooted in our inherent worth and value (or shallow roots) may result in no visible fruit or in fruit perishing prematurely in the face of uncertainty and challenges, as explained in the parable of the sower. A condemned heart may produce the things we do not desire or no fruit at all. We may also not produce any visible fruit if we attempt to produce our heart's desires through self-effort and persistent action without an awareness of the fact that we are not condemned and are indeed enough. The manifestation of lasting Kingdom fruit in the form of visible abundant relationships, finances, and physical soundness effortlessly springs forth as a physical manifestation in our lives as our heart and mind meditates on our desires while resting in our eternal value without exerting effort to obtain our desires outside of ourselves. As we seek first the Kingdom of God and His righteousness (which is also our righteousness), all other things will be granted unto us (Matthew 6:33) or spring forth in our lives. We have the ability to experience healing, wholeness, prosperity, and thriving relationships for ourselves and others. All things are yours (1 Corinthians 3:21)! When what we desire is more real to us on the inside to the extent that we are not concerned whether it ever manifests on the outside, we are ready to experience it in the natural realm, and it must come to pass.

4

YOU ARE NOT REJECTED!

I have learned not to allow rejection to move me.

—CICELY TYSON

Sometimes, we do not come into the realization of our own worthiness or create the life we desire because of our past and rejection. Past and even subsequent rejection may cause repeated thoughts of worthlessness to play over and over on the film of our minds and consequently life experience. These feelings and thought patterns of worthlessness or unrighteousness may cause us to experience further rejection and scarcity in our relationships, physical health, or finances. You may feel rejected based on external circumstances, but that is not your true identity. Your true internal identity has always been and will always be ACCEPTED. The design of rejection is to distort the reality of who we are, thereby causing us not to operate in or embrace our divinity.

We do not need to fear or despise rejection when we understand its true design and purpose. The true design of rejection is to propel you into God's purpose and plan for your life and the realization of who you really are. Anyone who outright rejects you was ultimately never meant to walk with you into your destiny and purpose, although their rejection can serve as a catalyst to propel you into your destiny and purpose. When we attempt to avoid rejection, we often have a way of experiencing it, anyway. Only when we are free to experience something will we be free from its effects. People were never meant to be our source of security or encouragement, so their rejection or even acceptance of us should be irrelevant. What we experience as rejection is indeed an illusion! How can you ever really be rejected when you are already accepted in the Beloved, and God is always with you? He is intertwined as you so it is impossible to be separated from Him. Since God is with you and for you, no one can ever truly be against you (Romans 8:31).

While your experience of rejection might be real, you don't have to dwell on feelings of guilt, shame, or unworthiness. You can choose to focus on feelings of love, appreciation, and your eternal acceptance in the face of apparent rejection. If utilized constructively, rejection causes us to dig deeper into our true identity and discover that we are in fact accepted, complete, and not in need of external affirmation or validation.

I do not want to minimize anyone's feelings of rejection. Most of us have encountered rejection in some form or another at some point in time. From early childhood until early adulthood, I spent many years of my life experiencing severe rejection to the point that I started a national suicide prevention hotline as an adult because I could relate to feelings of hopelessness. I experienced rejection from many of the people in my life, including within my household, extended family members on one side who favored my sister, peers, and others as a child, so I do understand the stinging pain it can produce.

If we are to ever step into our life's purpose, however, we must not allow rejection to master us, but we must learn how to master rejection by knowing who we are in the face of it. Rejection is simply a feeling of not being accepted based on external situations or circumstances. In fact, the more we focus on being excluded, the more we may further perpetuate circumstances that result in us being excluded, outwardly at least.

Remember, we are always accepted, regardless of what circumstances suggest. In my own life, repeated feelings of rejection in my formative years set up a subconscious program of shame, unworthiness, people pleasing, and inferiority for many years that manifested as perceived further rejection in my outward circumstances. I now understand though that outward circumstances do not define the inward reality of who I really am, which is accepted! I also understand that the past rejection I experienced created a vibration of rejection that I harbored, resulting in the manifestation of further rejection in my life.

The power to affect change always lies within us! Even if we feel or are actually physically alone, we are NOT rejected! In fact, when we understand who we are inwardly despite apparent rejection, outward circumstances will not even matter and then will begin to change. Additionally, when you understand who you truly are, the old feelings of rejection, unworthiness, guilt, condemnation, and shame will fade, and new feelings of acceptance, worth, righteousness, and confidence will emerge and flood your entire being.

Even if you feel that you have done something to cause you to be rejected, your true identity is always righteous and accepted, and you still deserve all of God's best by virtue of your identity.

We must have a very clear picture of who we are internally by submersing ourselves in truth. When we understand our true identity as eternal spiritual beings with infinite worth and value, we can rise above rejection and not feel inferior because of the rejection we have experienced in the past by someone else or may currently be experiencing based on what we perceive with our five physical senses or based on external circumstances. Our acceptance and righteousness transcend the sensory realm or external circumstances. More importantly, when we understand who we are internally, we will not doubt our value in the face of seeming rejection.

The key to thriving in the face of rejection is understanding that rejection is not a reflection upon who you are or your true identity. It does not matter who has rejected you. You were in the heart and mind of God before the foundation of the world! Often, we assign value to people and value their opinions based on our desire to be accepted by them. We allow their opinions to have a more prominent role in our lives than we should.

We don't have to accept someone's distorted perception of us as our reality!

Often, the persons who have been or are rejecting you are looking at you through a distorted lens based upon their own insecurities, fears, and deep-rooted low self-esteem issues. Additionally, sometimes the person or people that are rejecting you do so because they are intimidated by you and are more aware of your potential than even you are! In either case, being rejected does not define you or determine your value, as God alone defines you and determines your value, and He repeatedly states that your value is immeasurable and that you are emphatically righteous.

When you understand who you are and rise above rejection, you can embrace the love that has always been resonant inside of you with no need for external validation or to engage in people-pleasing behaviors to gain acceptance. Not only are you accepted, but you are also unconditionally loved. That unconditional love is not outside of you in the validation and opinions of others, but it is inside of you at all times. Other people's opinions do not define you. It is not how others may feel about you, whether good or bad, but it is how you think and feel about yourself that matters and produces manifestation in your life.

People Pleasing

People pleasing and the need to perform are often born out of the fear of rejection. They are usually cultivated early in life. People pleasing consists of performing to obtain the acceptance and love from other people that is ours by virtue of birth. It involves trying to obtain by effort that which we already have. People pleasing occurs when we look outside of ourselves to other people for affirmation of the acceptance and value that already reside within us. At the heart of people pleasing is the underlying internal fear that we are not enough and unworthy to receive acceptance unless we perform in some manner.

People pleasing can be detrimental, because it is utilized in order to obtain approval but may result in loss of true identity, which of course is divinity. I engaged in this behavior for a number of years during my youth. People pleasing, which is a form of approval addiction, essentially amounts to an individual placing the needs or desires of another person or persons above their own in an attempt to gain acceptance and validation. The behaviors and actions involved in people pleasing can include but are not limited to gift giving, docile agreement, not voicing one's opinion, avoiding conflict, trying to "fix" situations, and performing various acts to remain in an individual's good graces.

If the actions we take are out of fear of what people will think about us, they are always the wrong actions.

Attempting to "fix" situations may be one of the most common actions or behaviors associated with people pleasing.

The goals of people pleasing are often to avoid conflict, maintain peace, feel accepted—and most importantly—avoid rejection. Approval in the form of validation and acceptance is often the goal of people pleasing. People who have experienced excessive rejection often believe that they need the approval of others in order to avoid rejection, not realizing that they are always accepted as an eternal spiritual being with infinite worth and value. They have been conditioned to believe that they must perform to gain acceptance. They have also been conditioned to believe that if they experience rejection, there is something wrong with them or that they have done something wrong. A person feeling like they have done something wrong may experience a feeling of guilt within them and want to fix situations.

Guilt and Shame

People who have been conditioned to believe that they "are wrong" by virtue of their existence often experience a feeling of not only guilt but also shame. According to Wikipedia, "shame is an unpleasant self-conscious emotion typically associated with a negative evaluation of the self."[15] While guilt may be a fleeting emotion based on having committed a wrong, shame is a bit stronger. Wikipedia goes on to explain, "The experience of shame is directly about the self, which is the focus of evaluation. In guilt, the self is not the central object of negative evaluation, but rather the thing done is the focus."[16]

In essence, people who experience guilt may feel that they have done something wrong, while people who experience shame may feel that they are someone wrong. Guilt is a feeling while shame is a state or practiced feeling or emotion. People pleasing is often engaged in by people who have experienced excessive rejection in an attempt to alleviate not only rejection but also shame. People pleasers often reason that if they can please people and gain their approval, it will eliminate internal feelings of guilt and especially shame that may be the byproduct of years of rejection. The thought that people might think or talk badly about them is devastating to people pleasers. Essentially, their state of well-being is outsourced to the external and is contingent upon everyone liking them, thinking well of them, and not being angry at them, because they are terrified of the thought of facing yet another rejection! Shame attempts to also link us to perceived failed past performance on our part.

The Performance Trap

People pleasers often get caught in the aforementioned performance trap. They perform in various ways to gain the acceptance of other people. They often reason unconsciously that if they can just fix situations that they perceive are broken, or if they could just be "good enough," then perhaps everyone involved would be happy, not be upset with them, and accept them. You will always be "good enough" for the people who are meant to be in your life though!

Somehow, people pleasers always feel broken situations are their fault. They are committed to fixing situations that are quite often not even their fault. Their commitment to fix situations is less about finding mutual resolution among all parties involved than it is about alleviating their own internal tumultuous feelings of guilt and/or shame. They do not realize that they need never feel shame, despite outward circumstances. Pleasers may also partake of the performance trap not only through being a fixer but also through academic achievement, striving, passivity, and focusing excessively on their appearance. The performance trap is unhealthy, because there is always more striving that could be done. There is never enough action that can be taken to feel complete for pleasers, which can be emotionally agonizing. Without internal contentment, there is always just one more thing that can be done or fixed. Quite frankly, the performance trap can be physically and mentally exhausting!

Approval Addiction

In the article, "Approval Addiction: It's Impossible to Please Everyone," Life coach Amy Pearson notes, "People-pleasing is one kind of behavior that manifests as a result of being addicted to approval. But there are others. Some people seek approval by constantly trying to please others."[17] Essentially, people pleasing is one form of approval addiction.

Pearson goes on to say, "Others, like me, try to get approval by seeking out achievement and being the best at everything. I call these kinds of people 'performers.' Other kinds of approval addicts focus more on trying to win people over by blending in. These are the 'chameleons.' Others would rather just not be seen at all as to avoid any kind of rejection. These are the 'scaredy cats.'"[18]

All of the approval addicted behaviors Ms. Pearson mentions are an attempt to avoid rejection. The problem with the people pleasing form of approval addiction is that people who feel the need to please often sacrifice their integrity, preferences, and desires simply to be accepted by others and avoid the stinging pain of rejection. Often, people who have a history of experiencing rejection are prone to people pleasing just to secure or maintain peace and a place in the lives of others.

At the heart of all people pleasing, or even approval addiction, is a crippling concern about the thoughts of other people. In her book *Approval Addiction: Overcoming Your Need to Please Everyone*, author and teacher Joyce Meyer puts it this way, "If a person is an approval addict, he or she will have an abnormal concern and an abundance of thoughts about what people think of them."[19]

Approval addicts want people to think well of them. Approval addicts conclude that if people think well of them, they will be accepted and not rejected. We must not be concerned with the thoughts of other people but must be cognizant of the power of our own thoughts.

Contrary to popular belief, the thoughts of other people have no bearing on God's purpose and plan for your life! Your thoughts and internal speech about yourself have creative power and are what determine your destiny and future.

Your thoughts, no one else's, are what determine the trajectory of your life. Proverbs 23:7 is clear that as a man thinketh in his heart, so is he. As we think in our own heart, that is what our lives will be. Being concerned about the thoughts of other people or their opinions has no power in our lives unless we choose to give them attention and internalize the thoughts and opinions of others as our own. The negative thoughts and opinions of others are merely suggestions that we can choose to accept or reject. We do not have to agree with their negative opinions. Do not even entertain the criticism of others or their potential thoughts. We have a choice of whether we choose to dwell on and internalize the thoughts and opinions of others. Choosing to focus on the negative thoughts and opinions of others can produce death in various areas of our life, whereas focusing on God's positive estimate of us produces life, so it is important to choose life (Deuteronomy 30:19).

Immediately reject the negative thoughts and opinions of others concerning you and stay focused on God's assessment of you and His purpose and plan for your life, knowing that you are unconditionally loved and accepted by Him.

No amount of performing or people pleasing will ever help you feel valued by someone who is committed to not seeing your value and who does not even accept or value themselves. Don't allow someone else's distortion to become your reality. The sad truth is that many people who engage in rejecting others are often broken. Consequently, they view the world and other people through a tainted lens. It is not that they are rejecting you as much as they are really rejecting aspects of themselves.

A Word on Narcissists

People pleasers, who are often empaths, are often a magnet for people with personality disorders such as narcissism. When we do not understand who we are, we may attract people who exploit the knowledge we lack concerning our identity. I am sure many people reading this have heard or read about narcissism, as it seems to be very prevalent in our society today. In fact, you may even feel like you know someone who exhibits many narcissistic traits.

The Mayo Clinic succinctly defines narcissism as "a mental condition in which people have an inflated sense of their own importance, a deep need for excessive attention and admiration, troubled relationships, and a lack of empathy for others. But behind this mask of extreme confidence lies a fragile self-esteem."[20]

Similar to people pleasers or empaths, people with Narcissistic Personality Disorder (NPD) are also overly concerned with what people think about them and have not yet understood their inherent worth and value. However, unlike people pleasers, narcissists are often said to lack empathy and are not givers but are readily willing to exploit others in order to obtain the attention and validation they seek in order to feel worthy.

Empaths or pleasers who are not in tune with who they are may be sensitive to the thoughts and emotions of others and will often give off their time, bodies, energy, and resources in order to change the perceived negative thoughts and emotions of others and gain their acceptance. Pleasers may reluctantly engage in behaviors such as giving money, performing tasks, and even promiscuity in an attempt to feel accepted.

We must navigate life going forward with a clear understanding of who we are in order to avoid abuse from those who would attempt to exploit us and the emotional turmoil that ensues.

The Results of The People-Pleasing form of Approval Addiction

In friendships, relationships, and even romantic relationships, people pleasing may result in anxiety, abuse, emotional turmoil, and a lifetime of self-doubt for the person who engages in this form of approval addiction. In essence, people who seek to please others often lose themselves in the process. Not only that, they also often lose the ability to believe for life's best and to make their own decisions. Since they have often been conditioned to believe that the desires of others are more important than their own, they may not believe that they are worthy of receiving the things they truly desire. Additionally, since pleasers are also often instructed on how to fulfill the desires of others or of those they seek to please, they may reason that their opinions have no merit, and making simple decisions can prove challenging to them.

Not having a voice or speaking your own truth is a hallmark of people pleasing. We can agree to disagree with others while still speaking our truth in love. Relationships that do not bring life, peace, or good energy into our lives do not need to be tolerated. You are allowed to question or even terminate relationships where you are not allowed to have your own desires, have a voice, or make your own decisions.

Pleasers often seek the input of others before making important decisions and second-guess many decisions they make. They are conditioned to think that their opinions do not matter, are not to be expressed, or are flat out wrong. This belief may lead to many years of questioning themselves, emotional turmoil, and impaired identity. When things or relationships go "wrong," they usually believe it is their fault. Consequently, they grapple with what the right next step to take is and solicit everyone's input, because they are conditioned to believe that their own decision-making is flawed. They often outsource decisions to those around them who are outspoken and who are the perceived "experts" of life. Most of the decisions they solicit may involve how to "fix" fractured relationships in order to avoid feelings of being at fault and rejection. The self-doubt, guilt, and shame that ensue from questioning many decisions may take a physical and emotional toll on them, as it did in my own life, contributing to great bouts of anxiety and even physical ailments.

Essentially, they condemn themselves for any decision they make that they are later told or think was "wrong."

We must always remember that we are never condemned, eternally accepted, and perpetually righteous even when we make decisions that do not align with our true nature!

Anchored in Your Unchanging Identity!
People pleasing and approval addiction are dangerous because they place your sense of well-being and acceptance outside of yourself and in someone else's hands. The reason approval addiction is particularly dangerous is because external circumstances are fickle and always subject to change. A person may accept you one day and reject you the next. This creates unnecessary emotional

ups and downs in your life. People may accept you when you are pleasing to them but walk out of your life when you cease to benefit them or when you find your own voice and value.

Never accept feelings of guilt or shame to make someone else feel valuable, because those thoughts and emotions also create in your life and experience. It is impossible to please everyone, anyway, so why not rest in the truth of your eternal identity and acceptance? You are an autonomous being and do not have to accept feelings of rejection, guilt, or shame. When God created the world, when He had no one else to validate Him, He said that it was very good (Genesis 1:31).

We must learn to validate ourselves!

We must be anchored in the internal eternal unchanging identity of who we are. Second Corinthians 4:18 states, "While we do not look at the things which are seen, but at the things which are not seen. For the things which are seen are temporary, but the things which are not seen are eternal" (NKJV).

Our acceptance and value are non-negotiable and eternal!

We must stay focused on the internal unseen truths of our divinity, acceptance, value, and blamelessness granted by virtue of birth, as opposed to shifting external conditions such as the rejection of others. God has already accepted us, and we must choose to accept and validate ourselves. Additionally, allowing yourself to experience these feelings of worth and value will attract the abundant life that is your birthright.

Being The Star of Your Own Movie
YouTuber Aaron Doughty often talks about the importance of being the star of your own movie instead of seeking the approval of others and a role in their lives. We have all been created to "play a role," so to speak, on the screen of space and time with a very distinct destiny and purpose. People pleasers are often willing to sacrifice their own gifts and talents simply to have a role in the lives (or movie) of others.

In his video, "Stop Undervaluing Yourself and Overvaluing Others," and in many of his other videos, Doughty discusses the danger of placing other people on a pedestal and seeing yourself as inferior to them or falling into the role of being the cameo in everyone else's movie where you undervalue yourself.[21] If we undervalue ourselves to star in someone else's movie and tell ourselves the story that everyone is more valuable than ourselves, that is what will play out on the screen of space and time in our lives. He goes on to state that playing a cameo role in the lives of others occurs when we don't tap into our own value or see ourself as valuable already.[22]

While it is alright to value others, we must not undervalue ourselves in the process of attempting to gain approval and a place in their lives. Remember that you are always accepted without the need for external validation or approval. When you grasp the vastness of your completion, you will not be moved by people's rejection or even acceptance of you.

5

YOU ARE RIGHTEOUS!

> *I am convinced that the universe is under the control of a loving purpose and that in the struggle for righteousness man has cosmic companionship.*
>
> —Martin Luther King Jr.

Your identity from before the foundation of the world has always been righteous.

Righteousness is a state of being, not a state of doing.

Righteousness is the natural result of being one with the Almighty. Being righteous is what bestows your worth and entitles you to receive all of the bountifulness of God. You get to enjoy the desires of your heart out of your divinity, which is the Tree of Life's fruit. The Scriptures again are clear that we reign in life as we receive abundance of grace and the gift of righteousness (Romans 5:17). You were created to have dominion and to reign in life. When we are rooted in righteousness, everything works in our life.

Righteousness Defined

As noted in the preceding Scripture, righteousness is a gift. The Free Dictionary defines a gift as "something that is bestowed voluntarily and without compensation."[23] Righteousness is a free gift that flows out of grace and is not based on anything we do.

According to the Strong's Concordance, the word righteous in the Greek is the word "dikaios."[24] The concordance notes that "dikaios" means "equitable (in character or act); by implication, innocent, holy (absolutely or relatively)."[25] In essence, by virtue of being righteous, you can operate in innocence without guilt or shame of any kind, as if you had never sinned.

When we don't feel righteous or feel guilt or shame, it is hard for us to believe we deserve the desires of our heart and to receive them. On the other hand, when we operate in a state of righteousness, there are no limits to what we can receive.

No Limits

There are no limitations and no scarcity in the Spirit or the universe. There are billions of planets within our galaxy alone known as the Milky Way. Scientists now estimate that there are over a trillion galaxies in our universe, according to an article in *Forbes Magazine* entitled "This Is How We Know There Are Two Trillion Galaxies In The Universe."[26] There is no shortage in the universe or in our lives. Infinite resources are available for us to tap into as we align our hearts and minds to who we really are. There are also infinite ways and possibilities for us to receive the resources available to us. When we rest in a heart of righteousness, solutions that have always existed to our problems and resources that are in plain sight are unveiled. Chance encounters and serendipities occur, and perceived problems dissipate, as we focus on the truth of our identity.

Chance Encounters

A number of researchers have linked what essentially amounts to righteousness to increased instances of chance encounters. A 2011 *PsychCentral* article by Daniel Tomasulo entitled "Optimism and the Psychology of Chance Encounters" noted that a study where subjects, "imagined a 'best possible self' (BPS) for one minute and wrote down their thoughts generated a significant increase in positive affect. The researchers also concluded '. . . that imaging a positive future can indeed increase expectancies for a positive future.'"[27]

The article goes on to note that "we can change both how we feel in the moment and how we feel about what is to come. If we are prepared properly and are optimistic, we are likely to incorporate the chance encounter."[28]

Essentially, chance encounters may increase when we perceive a best possible self, which translates into perceiving our righteousness. These chance encounters may supply the resources and solutions we seek through a variety of ways.

Established in Righteousness

As stated previously in this book, we are not to attempt to struggle or fight against anything. There is only one fight that you will ever need to fight in your life. The Scriptures instruct us to fight only one fight, and that is the good fight of faith (1 Timothy 6:12).

The only fight of faith that you will ever have to fight is believing at all times and in all circumstances that you are righteous. For centuries, mankind has walked in a sin consciousness instead of a righteousness consciousness. Virtually all of the world's religions have started from the position of man's incompletion instead of wholeness. Many religions require rituals or performance of some sort to acquire right standing or favor with God. Sin consciousness often causes people to believe they are not worthy to receive the best of God. Sin or mistaken identity produces death, whether it is loss in our relationships, physical health, or finances. At times, we are unable to experience healing, wholeness, sound relationships, and abundance because we harbor mistaken identity and unworthiness in our hearts.

Your righteousness is not predicated on your "right or wrong" behavior but is the natural result of being one with the Almighty! A person, for example, who seldom argues, has never done drugs, or has never had sex outside of the institution of marriage, may still not experience the lasting fruit of their eternal righteous identity. If these preceding actions are derived out of self-effort or a condemned heart, they still may not produce the lasting fruit the person desires in their lives. True righteousness says, "I am complete, even if I recently had an argument with someone, just did drugs, or recently engaged in premarital sex." I will elaborate in a moment.

Your righteousness is not even based on your current circumstances, whether "good or bad." Righteousness also says that I am complete if I am homeless due to squandering resources, if I have a lump in my breast, or if I am pregnant outside of marriage. Righteousness has nothing to do with performance or circumstances but is the truth of who we inherently are. Righteousness says I am complete and righteous, whether I never get the house I desire, manifest healing, or obtain the social standing I desire. It doesn't worry about the outside at all but rests in the inside, and then the abundance of life has a way of appearing externally. We must be established in righteousness if we are to experience effortless manifestation.

People who derive their value from performance sometimes become upset when unconditional righteousness and God's grace are taught as stated in the preceding examples. The Pharisees and Sadducees of Jesus's day were steeped in religious performance in order to obtain right standing and favor with God, and many still are today. It is often said that God's grace is not a license to sin, oftentimes by individuals who derive their value from performance. Statements such as these can cancel out the good news that has gone forth concerning God's grace and immediately add a condition that puts the focus back on sin and places people back in bondage. The basis of our existence is freedom.

When people understand their wholeness and begin to no longer operate out of the need to obtain things outside of themselves, sin (mistaken identity) and the actions it produces will naturally dissipate.

The person who understands that they are abundant no longer needs to steal. The individual who understands that they are accepted no longer needs to engage in promiscuous behavior. The person who grasps that joy has been deposited on the inside of them no longer needs to partake of illicit drugs in an attempt to feel good. A consciousness of righteousness changes the trajectory of our lives. God's grace and the righteousness He bestows are unconditional and that should always be the focus of our lives, not sin!

You can be assured of your righteousness at all times, regardless of the opinions of others concerning you. You can also be assured of your righteousness, regardless of what you may have done that was not in line with your true identity a year ago, a day ago, or even a second ago! Every moment is a moment to begin anew. In each moment, you have the ability to focus on the gift of the present and create a fulfilling present moment and outcome not based on past performance.

Gold remains gold, whether it realizes it is gold or not. Gold also retains its value even if it falls in the mud. It is still gold. I have seen the devastation in peoples' lives from living in condemnation, which is the reason righteousness must be proclaimed!

Suicidal from Thoughts of Unrighteousness

For years, I took phone calls on the nonprofit suicide hotline I founded, Christian Suicide Prevention (CSP), along with numerous other volunteers. Often, the people who called from all over the nation struggled with thoughts of suicide based on a situation or circumstances in their lives. I often heard stories from people that they felt suicidal upon losing their job, their spouse filing for divorce, or contracting a sexually transmitted disease. Dwelling on condemning thoughts often made these people feel worse and compounded experiences of lack, loneliness, and sickness in their lives.

I was also struck that many of these individuals' feelings of condemnation preceded their current situation and were rooted in childhood after being abandoned, abused, or perpetually criticized. The theme of virtually every call I personally answered was the person's belief that they were not in right standing with God or had made an irreparable mistake.

Similarly, the antidote virtually every time was always the same in terms of hearing the message of their unchanging identity of righteousness, which resulted in them saying that they felt better by the end of the call. Knowing the truth is what sets us free!

I was hosting a radio program many years ago, and I interviewed a man who is now a Pastor who talked about feeling suicidal when he was young after his girlfriend at the time terminated their relationship. Although my spiritual understanding has evolved since that time, the audio interview is still available on the CSP website.[29] When the relationship ended, he went to one of the elevated "L" train platforms in Chicago to fall onto the train tracks and end his life. There was a feeling of condemnation after the termination of the relationship. Although he ultimately did not commit suicide after listening to a still small voice on the inside tell him to stop, he still tried to replace this feeling of condemnation with another girlfriend, alcohol use, and partying at the time. However, once he came into the understanding of the reality of his righteousness, he went on to meet a lovely woman that became his wife, had four lovely children, and became the pastor of a church. He experienced the desires of his heart once he understood who he really was.

All too often, though, many stories do not end like his. I also know of a man whom I attended college with who committed suicide—it is said—from feeling condemned after a romantic relationship ended. Similarly, I was stationed with another man overseas while I was serving in the Air Force who took his life after a relationship ended, it was again said. While there is no way to know for certain the reason these people chose to end their lives, it is prudent for us to proclaim the message of righteousness to others and understand our righteousness, regardless of the situations we find ourselves in or people's rejection.

Guard Your Heart

One of the main reasons I believe we should avoid certain people or situations is that if we are not yet rooted in our righteousness and allow encounters with them to produce condemning thoughts and emotions in our hearts and minds. We must guard our heart at all times in order to produce the fruit we desire in our lives. In fact, the Scriptures admonish, "Guard your heart above all else, for it determines the course of your life" (Proverbs 4:23 NLT).

What flows out of the heart manifests in our lives. Righteousness must become our dominant state in order for us to experience perpetual fruit in our lives and the lives of those around us. Do you remember the story about Jesus's disciple Peter walking on the water? As long as Peter stayed focused on his righteousness and his union with the Christ without condemnation, he was able to do the supernatural and walk on the water (Matthew 14:29). Nonetheless, as soon as he took his eyes off of this union, he began to sink (Matthew 14:30). We must learn to perpetually practice the feeling of love, righteousness, and no condemnation at all times and in all circumstances in order to transcend situations and circumstances.

Results of Righteousness

Being conscious of our righteousness will resurrect the dead places (fractured relationships, financial lack, and physical limitations) in our lives! Jesus was so conscious of His righteousness that He experienced resurrection from the dead. He did not condemn Himself as having done something wrong as He was being crucified (accept false guilt) but perpetually maintained a stance of righteousness in the face of death. As He is, so are we! The more we maintain a stance of righteousness, the more we will see the dead areas of our lives resurrected. You are not what other people say about you, what religion may say about you, or the potential challenges of your current circumstance. God's opinion of you is the only one that matters, and He perpetually declares that you are accepted and righteous! God's opinion of you is the only one that matters, not other people's, your past, or current situation.

6

YOU ARE A VISIONARY!

Vision is the art of seeing what is invisible to others.

—Jonathan Swift

Whether we are conscious of it or not, we are visualizing all the time. Many of us run our lives on autopilot by what we perpetually visualize. Operating on autopilot, so to speak, is good if the programming or the beliefs in our hearts are good and uplifting, but it can be detrimental if we are subconsciously navigating our lives based on condemning negative past programming. We think in images, not necessarily words. We have to reprogram the images in our hearts and minds in order to seamlessly experience different results in our lives if we are not experiencing what we desire.

In his book, *The Purpose Driven Life: What On Earth Am I Here For?*, Pastor Rick Warren compares the proclivity to dwell on subpar thoughts and images to a speedboat on autopilot headed east on a lake. In order to go west and change the direction of the boat, there are two options, he writes. First, you could try to change the direction of the boat by turning the steering wheel or helm with brute force. He goes on to say that this is a temporary solution, because after a short period of time, you will become tired and fatigued from utilizing your muscles to make this change. A better and more permanent solution is to reprogram the boat's autopilot to go in a western direction.[30] Similarly, we can attempt to change our lives by willpower or brute force, which will only produce momentary change. A better way to change our lives is through reprogramming our heart and imagining the life we desire. Reprogramming our internal self-talk and its associated images is vital to produce lasting change in our lives.

Often, we perpetuate cycles and attract undesirable outward situations because we have not healed inwardly or come to understand our true identity. Although we may not like the circumstances we perpetually find ourselves in, they often feel familiar to us. In essence, the image has never been changed on the inside, and we are still picturing things such as rejection and condemnation instead of acceptance and love. An inferior image that we perpetually harbor can sabotage our desires and future. This may explain, for example, the reason people who go on diets often regain the weight they lose and, in many cases, gain even more weight. Although they "desire" to be thin and lose weight, often, the inner image they continue to carry is of unworthiness and obesity. In order to produce lasting change, the image on the inside MUST be changed!

David's Internal Image Struggles

In an episode of the *Dr. Phil* show entitled, "Losing 400 Lbs., Gaining It All Back and More," for example, Dr. Phil interviewed a man named David. According to Dr. Phil's website, "At 26 years old, David was 600 pounds. At 31, David started exercising and eating right, and without gastric bypass surgery, David says he went from a dud to a stud losing 400 pounds in two years! However, David has transformed himself again, and now, the 43-year-old weighs 656 pounds."[31] David transformed himself and lost weight through sheer willpower. Nonetheless, since David's internal image of himself and his worthiness had not been transformed, his weight loss was short-lived, and he regained the weight he lost and more.

One of the most revealing aspects of the reason David failed to keep the weight off was in the following statement he made, "When I was that lower weight, people would say oh you look so good Dave, but in my mind, I felt like I wasn't good enough."[32] Although David honestly looked physically great, nothing had changed internally and, therefore, lasting change was not produced externally! David did not feel worthy to be thin and internally harbored images of unworthiness and obesity. Consequently, he regained the weight.

Worthiness and the proper images are vital in order to experience the change we desire in any area of our lives. When attempting to fix any problem such as poor health, financial lack, rejection, or relationship issues, we must first love ourselves in our current state and then internally picture the new image we would like to experience in order to see lasting change externally. If we condemn ourselves or the undesirable condition we find ourselves in, we will only produce more of it in our lives. Instead of relating more to the old image, we must focus on a new image of what we desire.

Reprogramming!

Reprogramming must take place in order to break toxic habits and create healthy ones, thereby attracting people and experiences in our lives that produce success and abundance.

A couple of ways to change negative patterns are through reprogramming our internal self-talk and associated images through meditation and habituation, both known as reconditioning therapy. Meditation is sometimes viewed by some people as solely an eastern practice, but the Scriptures also encourage meditation (Psalm 1:2–3). It is important for anyone who wants to experience success and abundance to meditate.

Meditation is simply dwelling on words and their associated images. In fact, we meditate all the time, whether we are conscious of it or not. Meditating on the things we don't desire in our lives can be defined as worry. It has often been said that if you know how to worry, then you know how to meditate. The more we dwell on certain words and images, the more they have a tendency to show up in our lives. Thus, meditation can be used in either a positive or negative way. We have a choice in terms of what we place our focus upon. The Scriptures admonishes us again, "Whatsoever things are honest, whatsoever things are just, whatsoever things are pure, whatsoever things are lovely, whatsoever things are of good report; if there be any virtue, and if there be any praise, THINK on these things" (Philippians 4:8). We have the power of what words and images we choose to accept into our thoughts or choose to reject. Although we may encounter negative situations, it is vital that we don't meditate on these experiences and instead place our attention on positive situations and what we do want to experience in our lives.

If we have had the proclivity to think on negative situations that place an emphasis on limitation and lack, then we must begin to think on ones that emphasize abundance and limitlessness. Like anything else, this takes practice. Just like with anything, though, seeing yourself and your life in a positive light can become second nature.

Habituation

Habituation is a form of reprogramming where you make a practice of repeating something every day over and over again. Just as toxic thought patterns and images are often slowly programmed into our subconscious by parental figures, peers, and others over time, positive thought patterns and images can be slowly programmed into our subconscious over time as well. Some people practice habituation through "I AM" affirmations. Whatever you desire to experience positively in your life, you would say that you are those things, because you indeed already are those things. I AM affirmations serve as a reminder of the wholeness and completeness you were created to experience. When we raise our consciousness to who we are and were created to be, we often attract those things effortlessly into our lives.

Positive I AM short phrases might include statements such as, "I am strong, I am successful, I am wealthy, I am a CEO, I am a wife, I am beautiful," among many other things. I AM affirmations can be repeated once a day, twice a day, or multiple times per day. These affirmations and statements begin to form new desirable thoughts and images in the heart and mind. What is important is to repeat these I AM statements whenever thoughts of lack and limitation come to mind. As you repeat positive I AM affirmations and thoughts of lack and limitation begin to subside, you can make fewer of these statements as they become increasingly etched in your heart and a natural part of your programming. As these statements become etched in your heart, you will embody these statements and no longer need to repeat them as frequently.

Positive habituation may also include I AM sentences such as "I AM wealthy and succeed in everything I put my hand to." Positive habituation is important for anyone who endeavors to experience more abundance or success in their life.

Tony Robbins's Habituation Statement

Motivational speaker extraordinaire and author Tony Robbins equates much of his success to the habitual affirmations he stated over and over before he became a million-dollar influencer. He would say certain affirmations over and over for thirty minutes. In his YouTube video "Focus on Yourself Not Others," Robbins notes that his daily affirmation was, "God's wealth is circulating in my life. His wealth flows to me in avalanches of abundance. All my needs, desires, and goals are met instantaneously by infinite intelligence. I'm one with God and God is everything."[33]

According to Robbins, rituals equal results. The important part of habituation is ensuring you make a habit of repeating desired statements until image transformation occurs and ultimately you embody the statement(s) you have been making.

Meditation
Meditation is also an important way to change our internal programming, as previously mentioned. Meditation is total concentration on a single train of thought, including its associated images. Essentially, it is seeing the truth of who we are in our mind's eye. Meditation does not try to force things to occur but focuses on the fact that they have already occurred and have been deposited on the inside of us and that we already are all that we desire.

Meditation should be enjoyable and should not feel like effort. If it feels like effort, you may be trying too hard to bring about the external outcome you desire with your own strength. Some people may also use terms such as visualization when describing meditation. While meditation is usually associated with quieting the mind and being aware of the present moment, visualization "involves picturing in your mind the outcome of something before it's happened."[34]

In essence, meditation concerns the present, whereas visualization is about the future. Meditation and visualization are most effective when the mind and body are relaxed. The best time to meditate or visualize, as previously noted, are immediately before falling asleep or immediately upon waking up. During this time, the brain is in a theta wave state. According to the website Brain Sync, theta is an ideal state for super learning, storing information in long-term memory, and reprogramming your subconscious mind.[35] The site goes on to explain that because theta brainwave activity is associated with heightened receptivity, "It is the ideal state to reprogram your mind with positive thoughts that assist in changing habits and behaviors."[36] Theta is the mind state that many believe allows us to ultimately alter perceptible reality.

Many sages and enlightened thinkers throughout the course of time have long known the importance and benefits of meditation and visualization. Concerning the "blessed man," the Scriptures note, "His delight is in the law of the Lord, and in His law he meditates day and night. He shall be like a tree Planted by the rivers of water, that brings forth its fruit in its season, whose leaf also shall not wither; and whatsoever he does shall prosper" (Psalm 1:2–3 NKJV).

The passage is clear that those who meditate and implant prosperous images into their subconscious mind or heart will produce fruit or experience prosperous lives. A prosperous life is up to us. Meditation and visualization are almost inextricably linked, since the future outcome that we desire (visualization) is also our present spiritual reality (meditation). As stated throughout this book, it is important for us to rest in the realization of who were created to be and already are as we visualize and feel the life we desire to experience. This life has already been provided for us.

Reprogramming such as meditation and habituation are even more imperative for those who need to replace a lifetime of negative programming, self-condemnation, and abuse with positive images in order to walk in the reality of their desires. At times, we may need to even remove ourselves from condemning environments in order for the images we harbor to be properly replaced with prosperous ones.

The Importance of Visualization

Many influential and wealthy individuals of our time believe that good internal programming produces good results! America's success coach Jack Canfield discusses how he used positive visualization and feeling states to attract his multimillion-dollar empire as a speaker, author, and success coach. In his blog, "Visualization Techniques to Affirm Your Desired Outcomes: A Step-by-Step Guide," Canfield notes that visualization techniques have been used by many successful people over the years such as himself to attract wealth and success.

Canfield writes that "the practice has given some high achievers what seems like superpowers, helping them create their dream lives by accomplishing one goal or task at a time with hyper focus and complete confidence. In fact, we all have this awesome power, but most of us have never been taught to use it effectively. Elite athletes use it. The super-rich use it. And peak performers in all fields now use it. That power is called visualization. The daily practice of visualizing your dreams as already complete can rapidly accelerate your achievement of those dreams, goals, and ambitions."[37]

Notice that Canfield emphasizes that we should visualize our dreams as ALREADY COMPLETE! It has been said that our lives go in the direction of our most dominant thought, which is true, but our lives also go in the direction of our most dominant image. Our dominant thought and image should always be that we are complete!

7

YOU ARE A CO-CREATOR!

*I believe that the heart is the most forceful,
impactful element in our lives.*

—Maya Angelou

We have been gifted with the ability of co-creation as we focus on our union with the Eternal One. We were created to create. Our thoughts and feelings mold and shape our reality. We have been given the unique gift to imagine the life we desire. What you see in your imagination is just as real as anything that exists physically. No one has ever built anything in the physical realm until they first had a blueprint or image of it. Your imagination is the blueprint to the life of your dreams.

Feel its Reality Now!

Many enlightened thinkers have stated that affirmations or meditation must be accompanied by the feeling state of your end goal. Essentially, it is important to allow yourself to experience the feelings that you believe your desired outcome will generate long before it materializes.

As previously noted, the primary reason you desire anything in life is to feel the feelings you believe will be generated within you once you obtain those things. For example, you may desire a million dollars because of the feeling of freedom it would generate inside. You might desire a new luxury vehicle because it might symbolize success and generate feelings of wealth for you. Or finally, you might desire a romantic relationship because you would then allow yourself to feel love. The truth is, love is already resonant within you, wealth is already within you, and freedom is already on the inside of you as a divine being, and you can give yourself permission to feel those feelings from your heart now before the materialization of your desires.

Your Heart's Power

Your heart is one of the most powerful tools on the planet. It is the first organ to develop after conception, and it plays a vital role throughout our lives, pumping blood throughout every cell of our bodies. The heart also has the ability to beat after the brain is dead. The heart is said to beat automatically "about 100,000 times in one day and 35 million times in a year. During an average lifetime, the human heart will beat more than 2.5 billion times."[38] Not only does the heart assist in nourishing every cell of our body through its blood and consequently oxygen distribution, but its reach also extends well beyond our physical body. The heart supplies life to our organs, tissues, and cells through its blood distribution, but it also supplies life to our dreams and desires through its electromagnetic field.

The Heart Remembers and Feels

The heart "has 40,000 neurons and the ability to process, learn, and remember."[39] Essentially, your heart has a brain of its own. The neurons in the heart can also sense and feel.[40] In fact, there are many stories of the heart's ability to remember and feel, with heart transplant patients supporting the reality of its infinite intelligence. There was the story of a woman who "was given a heart transplant and upon recovering, realized she suddenly had an insatiable craving for KFC's fried chicken and green peppers ... Upon conducting some personal investigating, she managed to find out who her donor was and contacted his family. During the conversation she had with them, they shared with her that his favorite foods were KFC's fried chicken and green peppers.'"[41]

An even more compelling story about the heart's feeling and remembrance mechanism is noted below:

> The most powerful case that exists by far is about an 8-year-old girl who received the heart of a 10-year-old girl who had been violently murdered. The 8-year-old girl kept having a recurring nightmare, ever since receiving her new heart. The nightmare was always about a man chasing her in the woods and hurting her. The nightmare became so paralyzing that they took her to see a counselor, who concluded she had to be describing an actual event. Upon connecting the transplant to the timing of the nightmares, they decided to let the girl recount the details of this event to law enforcement, such as time, place, clothing, and the exact words the girl said to the man in the dream when he was hurting her. Unbelievably, the information led them to an arrest and eventually to the conviction of her murderer. It turned out that the words the 8-year-old kept dreaming about were actually the 10-year-old's last words, as the killer confirmed.

> This little girl's heart stored the memory of her attack and passed it on to her heart's recipient, which ultimately solved the crime.[42]

These stories are positive proof that the heart has the ability to remember and feel. Your heart is not limited to feeling and sensing the past, though; it can also feel right now to mold your future.

Your Heart Is Magnetic
Energy literally is everything, and the energy of the heart is massive. The heart is said to have an "electrical component about 60 times greater" than the brain's and "an electromagnetic energy field 5000 times greater than the brain's."[43] Your heart is quite literally magnetic! The heart's magnetic "energy is said to reach about three feet outside of the physical body and can be detected in another person sitting nearby via an electrocardiogram (ECG)," but scientists also concede that "the potential of how far our heart's electromagnetic energy field can reach continues to be studied as technology plays catch-up."[44]

Many contemporary scholars believe that there is no limit to how far your heart's energetic field reaches. Not only can other people feel your heart's energy, but your heart's energy can also be detected within others. Our heart emanates massive amounts of energy based on our thoughts and feelings, thereby changing and rearranging things around us. This may explain the reason that our thoughts and feelings have a way of forming our reality. The electromagnetic energy field that emanates from our heart has a way of reaching not only the people around us, as noted above, but the things around us as well. People and things with similar energies will resonate with the energy our hearts emanate and be attracted into our life experience. Literally, as you *THINK IN YOUR HEART,* so are you (Proverbs 23:7), or so will your experience be.

Energy is Everything

In recent years, the field of quantum physics has gained increased attention and prominence. Within this field of study, the notion that everything is indeed energy has gained increasing acceptance. The idea that everything is composed of energy and not physical matter is not new. In fact, Albert Einstein stated, "Everything is energy, and that's all there is to it. Match the frequency of the reality you want, and you cannot help but get that reality. It can be no other way. This is not philosophy. This is physics," according to Educate, Inspire, Change.[45]

We can do as Einstein suggested and match the frequency of the reality we desire through our heart's thoughts and feelings. In essence, everything is energy, and like energy attracts like energy.

We can activate the invisible quantum field that surrounds us with our heartfelt emotions.

Solid matter, as we once understood it in terms of being comprised of atoms and subatomic particles, does not really exist, it is now thought, according to physicists. In fact, it has been noted that "solid matter as we conventionally understand it does not exist in the universe. For all particles are merely vibrations of energy."[46]

Vibrations of energy form all that we can physically see, hear, taste, touch, and smell. Noted physicist Niels Bohr put it this way, "If quantum mechanics hasn't profoundly shocked you, you haven't understood it yet. Everything we call real is made of things that cannot be regarded as real."[47]

In essence, what is more real is the energetic field that we cannot see and not the things that we can physically see. That energetic field is called the spiritual realm, and we have the ability at any moment to tap into that field or realm.

The Heart of The Matter

The preceding article goes to the heart of our true identity. The article notes, "Everything is energy, including you. All that you are is energy, and when you start to perceive yourself in this way, as an almost 'spiritual' being untouched by space and time, and unrestricted by an apparently physical body, the barriers within you will begin to dissipate . . . Based on this knowledge what we are at our essence is a vibrational being made up of pure energy, and collectively as the human race how we vibrate creates the reality around us."[48]

In essence, who you are at your core is a spiritual being. As such, you have the ability to shape and mold the world around you into the reality you desire to experience. You are not your past, you are not your perceived limitations, but what you are is a spiritual being with infinite transformational power. Reality is not static based on our past failures or shortcomings but is ever changing and yielding at all times based on the power that we utilize within us now in this moment. The thoughts and feelings of your heart shape your reality.

Joseph Murphy poignantly puts it this way: "Thought fused with feeling becomes a subjective faith or belief, and according to your belief is it done unto you. Matthew 9:29."[49]

Your beliefs (heartfelt thoughts and feelings) create your reality. The Scriptures aptly note, "Therefore I tell you, whatever you ask for in prayer, believe that you have received it, and it will be yours" (Mark 11:24 NIV). This verse encourages us to believe that we have already received what we desire before it comes into physical being by seeing it and feeling it. God has given us this ability. We must see in our mind's eye the realness of our desires, because they are an energetic or spiritual reality. Seeing yourself walking in your desires and feeling the emotions of it while understanding your worthiness to receive is the art of true prayer.

Miracle Through Feeling Prayer

Author and speaker Gregg Braden has often noted in his seminars and videos a miracle that occurred at what is known to westerners as the Medicineless Hospital (Zhineng Qigong) in China through what amounts to feeling prayer. Braden shows a video in his seminars and videos of a woman "with a cancerous three inch diameter tumor in her bladder," and practitioners at the healing center are "trained to feel just the precise feeling in their hearts—they create the feeling as if the woman is already healed. We get to look inside her body through a sonogram and watch her cancer disappear in three minutes."[50]

Essentially, the practitioners feel the excitement of the woman being healed and her wholeness, and within minutes—not weeks or even days—her tumor completely dissolves, and she experiences the physical manifestation of a healing. Gregg Braden has been noted as saying that "the feeling is the prayer."[51]

While some might be skeptical about the validity of this account, the premise is the same one found in Mark 11:24 previously noted. We feel the feeling of what we desire—in this case, healing and wholeness—and experience its reality because it is already ours.

There are three important takeaways from the woman who is said to have been healed in this account that I believe can be applied in our own lives. First, like the practitioners, we do not need to judge ourselves as having done something wrong to be in the situation we find ourselves or judge the situation itself as evil. Remember from earlier statements in this book that what we judge we empower, and judging things as evil often prevents life from flowing into the situation. Second, our current circumstance or state is one possibility out of many possibilities that could occur, and we can simply choose a new possibility of wholeness and abundance. All things are literally possible, and all possibilities already exist now. We focus on what we desire and not what we do not desire without trying to figure out exactly how our desire will come about in the natural realm. We must just stay focused on our end goal. Finally and most importantly, of course, we can just briefly see ourselves abundant and whole in our mind's eye and feel the thrill of that reality now, and it must come into physical being. We do not have to question "will it work" when we seek to manifest our desires but rest in the fact that it has already worked. Not only will it work, but it is already done. All things we desire exist now and are real.

My Experience

I know that, in my own life, I have experienced a steady stream of clients, growth in my business, and the dissipation of health challenges as I have applied these principles and rested in my unchanging eternal identity of righteousness. I have also attracted friendships and relationships of a different caliber than I did in the past as I have meditated on my worthiness and not the rejection and shame that many in my life close to me tried to instill in me growing up. Realizing that all things are literally available to me and have already been supplied has radically transformed my life and many other people I encounter. If you think you cannot experience your heart's desires, then you probably will not. If you think that you can, all things are literally possible and available to you now!

8

YOU ALREADY ARE . . .

Don't be afraid to give yourself permission to be great and never dim your light for anyone.

—Dawn J Epting

You already are whatever you desire to be. Reread this book as often as necessary until its truth are settled in your heart. You can plant seeds right now in this moment to write the rest of your story and feel its reality out of a righteous and worthy heart. The pen is in your hand to write your story unrestrained by past obstacles or future concerns.

In fact, feel free to take the available space of the remaining page(s) of this chapter to write your heart's desires in terms of the life you would like to experience, if you are reading the paperback version of this book. You can also take a sheet of paper and write your story as well, referring to it often and revising it as your dreams expand.

You might even want to consider rewriting your past, as explained in Chapter 2 of this book, in addition to your desired present and future, of course. You have everything in this moment to experience the life of your dreams; in fact, you always have!

Remember to never doubt your value, because you are, have always been, and will always be more than enough!

YOUR NEW STORY BEGINS NOW . . .

NOTES

Chapter 1.
1. "Chata," Bible Study Tools, https://www.biblestudytools.com/lexicons/hebrew/nas/chata.html.
2. "Miracle," Dictionary.com, https://www.dictionary.com/browse/miracle.
3. Dana Hunsinger Benbow, "Cheerleader Was Quadriplegic After 2016 Gymnastics Accident. Now She's Walking." *USA Today*, October 6, 2019. https://www.usatoday.com/story/sports/2019/10/06/cheerleader-quadriplegic-after-gymnastics-accident-2016-now-walking/3870203002/.
4. Ibid.
5. "Heal Your Body With Your Mind: Dr. Joe Dispenza," Lewishowes.com, https://lewishowes.com/podcast/heal-your-body-with-your-mind-dr-joe-dispenza/.
6. Ibid.

Chapter 2.
7. "4 Ways to Change Your Thoughts," Brucelipton.com, https://www.brucelipton.com/blog/4-ways-change-your-thoughts.
8. Joseph Murphy, *The Power of Your Subconscious* Mind (Joseph Murphy, Kindle ed.), 20.

9   Ibid, p.18.
10 Joseph Prince, *Destined to Reign* (Tulsa: Harrison House Publishers, 2007), 129.
11 Ibid, p. 130–131.
12 Mike Popovich, "The Parable of The 'Unrighteous Servant' – The Creative Power of Forgiveness," YouTube, https://www.youtube.com/watch?v=C1fn6UYSjf8.
13 Kay Fairchild, "Living Out of Our Spiritual Resources #1," YouTube, https://youtu.be/h4Phv2gFL6k.

Chapter 3.
14 Gregg Braden, *Secrets of the Lost Mode of Prayer* (United States: Hay House Publishers, 2006), 88.
15 Ibid, p. 88.

Chapter 4.
16 "Shame," Wikipedia.com, https://en.m.wikipedia.org/wiki/Shame.
17 Ibid.
18 Amy Pearson, "Approval Addiction: It's Impossible to Please Everyone," ProjectKnow, https://www.projectknow.com/approval-addiction-you-just-cant-please-everyone/.
19 Ibid.
20 Joyce Meyer, *Approval Addiction: Overcoming Your Need to Please Everyone* (Hodder & Stoughton, Kindle ed).
21 "Narcissistic Personality Disorder," Mayoclinic.com, https://www.mayoclinic.org/diseases-conditions/nar-

cissistic-personality-disorder/diagnosis-treatment/drc-20366690.
22 Aaron Doughty, "Stop Undervaluing Yourself and Overvaluing Others," YouTube, https://www.youtube.com/watch?v=0vvyWlla8Zo.
23 Ibid.

Chapter 5.
24 "Gift," FreeDictionary.com, https://www.thefreedictionary.com/gift.
25 James Strong, *Strong's Concordance* (Nashville: Thomas Nelson Publishers, 1990), 23.
26 Ibid.
27 Ethan Siegel, "This Is How We Know There Are Two Trillion Galaxies In The Universe," *Forbes*, October 18, 2018. https://www.google.com/amp/s/www.forbes.com/sites/startswithabang/2018/10/18/this-is-how-we-know-there-are-two-trillion-galaxies-in-the-universe/amp/.
28 Daniel Tomasulo, "Optimism and the Psychology of Chance Encounters," *PsychCentral*, January 5, 2011. https://psychcentral.com/blog/optimism-and-the-psychology-of-chance-encounters#1.
29 Ibid.
30 Christian Suicide Prevention, http://www.christiansuicideprevention.com/.

Chapter 6.

31 Rick Warren, *The Purpose Driven Life: What On Earth Am I Here For?* (Grand Rapids: Zondervan, 2004).

32 "Losing 400 Lbs., Gaining It All Back and More," Dr. Phil.com. https://www.drphil.com/shows/losing-400-lbs-gaining-it-all-back-and-more/.

33 Ibid.

34 Tony Robbins, "Focus On Yourself Not Others," YouTube, https://www.youtube.com/watch?v=zoe_ea-2Z8us.

35 "Visualization Meditation," Headspace.com, https://www.headspace.com/meditation/visualization.

36 "Theta Binaural Beats," Brainsync.com, https://www.brainsync.com/collections/theta-binaural-beats.

37 Ibid.

38 "Visualization Techniques to Affirm Your Desired Outcomes: A Step-by-Step Guide," Jackcanfield.com, https://www.jackcanfield.com/blog/visualize-and-affirm-your-desired-outcomes-a-step-by-step-guide/.

Chapter 7.

39 "Amazing Heart Facts," PBS.org, https://www.pbs.org/wgbh/nova/heart/heartfacts.html.

40 Jessica I. Morales, "The Heart's Electromagnetic Field Is Your Superpower." *Psychology Today*,

November 29, 2020, https://www.psychologytoday.com/us/blog/building-the-habit-hero/202011/the-hearts-electromagnetic-field-is-your-superpower.

41 HeartMath LLC, Contributor, "Let Your Heart Talk to Your Brain," Huffington Post, December 6, 2017. https://www.huffpost.com/entry/heart-wisdom_b_2615857.

42 Jennifer Chase, "Your Heart Has Its Own Mind." Medium.com, February 20, 2019. https://medium.com/@jenniferchase_45595/your-heart-has-its-own-mind-5d2143d8849.

43 Ibid.

44 Morales, "The Heart's Electromagnetic Field Is Your Superpower."

45 Ibid.

46 Kash Khan, "Everything is Pure Energy, Including You. Change It And You Will Change The World." Educate, Inspire, Change, October 12, 2015. https://educateinspirechange.org/everything-is-pure-energy-including-you-change-it-and-you-will-change-the-world/.

47 Ibid.

48 Ibid.

49 Ibid.

50 Murphy, *The Power of Your Subconscious Mind*.

51 "Transcript From Gregg Braden's Science of Healing Workshop," The Way of Meditation, October

5, 2015, https://www.thewayofmeditation.com.au/healing-of-tumour-using-qi-gong.

52 Gregg Braden, "How Do You Pray?" Heal Your Life, July 25, 2016. https://www.healyourlife.com/how-do-you-pray.

ABOUT THE AUTHOR

Dawn Epting is a visionary author, speaker, the Chief Executive Officer of the Nonprofit Development Center (NPDC), and founder of Christian Suicide Prevention (CSP). CSP was the nation's first faith-based crisis hotline and has assisted thousands of people throughout the nation since 2011. The NPDC assists for-profit and nonprofit companies through business coaching, nonprofit implementation and expansion, and business planning. Dawn delivers speeches that encompass understanding identity, suicide prevention, and business. Dawn obtained a Master of Business Administration (MBA) from Southern Illinois University Edwardsville (SIUE) and a Bachelor of Arts in History from the University of Maryland, University College, while serving in the US Air Force in Ramstein, Germany, as a Budget Analyst. Her military tour took her to such places as California, Korea, and Germany.

Dawn has spoken in various locations around the globe and taught courses at churches for women concerning maximizing their potential as well as courses for both men and women. Her speeches and teachings draw from a wealth of experience obtained from the numerous years she served in the US Air Force, NPDC and CSP oversight, faith, and from illnesses and emotional challenges she has experienced and overcome in her own life by the grace of God.

In the book *365 Days of Grace*, available on Amazon, Dawn encourages individuals to walk in the grace of God and live free from guilt and condemnation!

In her latest book, *Never Doubt Your Value: You Are More Than Enough*, also available on Amazon, Dawn encourages individuals to understand their eternal worth and value, regardless of situations or circumstances.

BOOK SUMMARY

Life is not so much about obtaining as it is about discovering—that which we have been looking for externally but have always possessed internally! Once we discover what we possess inside, we will effortlessly receive all of life's abundance instead of striving hard to obtain it. When we truly awaken to who we are, and have always been, there will be no limits to what we can receive in terms of abundance in relationships, finances, health, business endeavors, or dreams!

Often we must be reminded of who we truly are! We are not our past, we are not the rejection we experienced, we are not how people have negatively tried to define us, and we are not incomplete. We were created complete, accepted, righteous, and visionaries with unlimited creative abilities to transform the world around us! The more we rest in the true knowledge of who we are and have always been, the more we will walk in the experience of the things we desire for our lives and the lives of those around us! In essence, manifestation will be effortless. Our worth has never been in question or fluctuated. It is the awareness of our immeasurable worth that we may need to discover!

www.ingramcontent.com/pod-product-compliance
Lightning Source LLC
Chambersburg PA
CBHW031256290426
44109CB00012B/601